Unexpected.

25 Daily Advent Devotionals

By Danielle Ripley-Burgess

Book Design & Illustration by Will Bryan.

WillBryanDesign.com

ISBN 9781731136916

To Mike:

My first book cannot be dedicated to anyone other than my biggest fan. You show me love and light. God's going to take care of us.

Table of Contents

A topical study of selections from Scripture based on the advent story.

Acknowledgments

The first devotional book I ever owned came from my mom shortly after I became a Christian; if memory serves me correctly, we bought it at a garage sale and I devoured it each night before I went to bed. Thank you, Mom, for planting the seed and for constantly supporting me. The Heart of America Christian Writers Network (HACWN) gave me my first opportunities to write and feel the amazing accomplishment of getting published. I'll forever be grateful for you. Thank you Doc, Amy and Mike for proofing and being my editors. Will, you made this book come alive with art; I think we should nickname it "Earl." Kevin, you introduced me to Dana, who gave me confidence in self-publishing. Ashlyn, you inspire me to write and reach the next generation. Mae, you're the reason I've forced myself to sit down, write and publish. This book is from my heart to yours. Barbara, your challenge to experience advent in a way I'd never known up until a few years ago is one of countless ways you've changed my life. Jesus, I pray this book honors you and our story. Thank you for your unexpected light that always outshines my darkness.

Dear Friend,

I love surprise parties, random adventures, and spur-of-the-moment ideas. But "whimsy" isn't exactly my middle name. Especially during the holidays.

Typically around this time of year, I'm co-dependent on wish lists, party reminders, and color-coded calendars. I'm focused on arriving on time with yummy appetizers, trays of treats, and white elephant gifts in hand. Although my organization can be helpful, it can also be a barrier for the unplanned and unexpected. Yet this is how the first advent began.

The birth of Christ didn't come on a penciled-in date where everyone cleared their calendars. He wasn't born into circumstances that were budgeted for, nor did He arrive at, what His parents considered, a convenient time in their lives.

Christ was born when God said it was time.

> *"But when the fullness of time had come, God sent forth his Son, born of woman, born under the law, to redeem those who were under the law, so that we might receive adoption as sons," (Galatians 4:4-5).*

Most of us accept that God's timing isn't our timing, but advent challenges us to come face to face with how we handle the unexpected.

If you've never read the Christmas story, I encourage you to read the first two chapters of Matthew and Luke in the Bible. It will introduce key people and events that make up this wonderful story. We're going to walk through advent topically, not chronically, but this background is an important primer.

Let's journey together to uncover how monotonous routines bring beautiful situations, annoying interruptions serve as invitations, and hearts of adoration invite powerful transformation. The baby we didn't expect changes everything.

- Danielle

The Unexpected
Magic of the Mundane

In the places we faithfully follow routine, God shows up. In our plans and commitments, in age-old liturgies and holiday traditions, we set the stage for breakthrough. Advent starts here: in the mundane and the simple, the routine and the regular. Although we don't expect it, this is where the natural turns supernatural; where the ordinary becomes extraordinary.

On Duty

"Now while he [Zechariah] was serving as priest before God when his division was on duty..." (Luke 1:8).

Sometimes, the most powerful thing we do is wake up and show up. There's hidden power in punching in and logging on. Our commitment to continue doing what we did yesterday is not lost on God. When we report for duty, He notices. He honors our commitments. He likes to surprise us in them.

Zechariah and Elizabeth kick off the advent story. Zechariah, a priest, showed up to work one day and was chosen to enter the temple and offer the sacrifices. It was a special, yet typical, role for a priest. But the normal became abnormal when he stood face to face with the angel Gabriel inside of the temple. God's 400-year silence was broken. The angel delivered a life-changing message. God heard his prayers and his infertile wife would soon become pregnant. God was doing a miracle. The son that would be born was to be called "John," and serve as the "forerunner" to the long-awaited Messiah.

It's easy to forget God is a God of miracles, and it's even easier to stop expecting them when we're caught up in day-to-day routines and monotony. Yet advent invites us to view our schedules in a different way and see them as an invitation and opportunity for God to appear.

{ *Prayer: Lord, help me experience you in my daily routine. Amen.*

Summons

"In those days a decree went out from Caesar Augustus that all the world should be registered," (Luke 2:1).

W ho is calling for us right now? Is someone requesting our presence? Are we expected to be somewhere at a certain time and place? Do we want to go, or would we rather bundle up, sit alone and watch movies?

When the emperor Caesar Augustus called for a census, a Jewish man named Joseph and his fiancée, Mary, were expected to travel to his hometown of Bethlehem, the City of David. For a woman in her final weeks of pregnancy, I'm certain she had many reasons to avoid the trip. Yet despite the son of God being in her womb, none of them outweighed the summons. They had to go. They packed up, made the trek, and arrived in a crowded city where the only place to lie down (and give birth) was a dirty animal barn. Yet as a result, decades of longstanding prophecy came true. The baby Jesus was born in the City of David—just as the prophet Micah foretold (Micah 5:2).

Sometimes, especially during the holidays, our presence is requested, but we don't want to go. Yet like Mary and Joseph, sometimes we must press in and not dismiss an important summons. We can trust that wherever we go, God will work out His master plan.

{ *Prayer: Lord, show me where to go so my life aligns with your plan. Amen.*

Keep Watching

"And in the same region there were shepherds out in the field, keeping watch over their flock by night," (Luke 2:8).

I'm not tending sheep right now, and it's unlikely you are too. But, we're both keeping watch. We're watching our homes, families and friends to ensure the people we love feel cared for and safe. We're watching our bodies to keep them healthy. We're watching our budgets as we purchase gifts and keep our accounts balanced. We're watching our calendars to ensure we schedule and arrive on time. In this diligent watching, advent appears.

The shepherds working the fields weren't expecting a face-to-face angelic encounter as the sun went down and their nighttime duties kicked in. But their careful watchfulness made them attentive listeners who became some of the first witnesses to the birth of Christ. While watching over their sheep, God broke up their mundane routines with unexpected news. The Savior of the world, the long-awaited Messiah, had just been born.

As we find ourselves in the advent story, may we trust that our watching will also lead to encounters with Him.

{ *Prayer: Lord, help me encounter you as I watch over all you've entrusted to me. Amen.*

Humble Beginnings

"For he [the Lord] has looked on the humble estate of his servant,"
(Luke 1:48).

It's easy to get discontent during the holidays and distracted by comparison. Social media feeds us adorable photos of others' traditions and gifts. Neighbors' twinkling trees and outdoor decorations encourage an unspoken race to keep up. We can get so lost in striving to be perfect and impressive, we take our hand off humility—the way of Christ. We forget God's attraction to humble beginnings.

God chose Mary to carry the Savior of the world within her womb. This is significant. God didn't choose an emperor's wife to bear His son. He also didn't look for the envy of the neighborhood nor a royal queen to mother Jesus. He chose a young, faithful girl who identified as His humble servant. God counted her worthy to conceive a perfect, holy child.

God looks beyond our earthly roles and into our hearts. He uses hearts that honor humble beginnings and strip themselves of pride. He's not looking for famous rockstars or wealthy debutants to carry His message, He's looking for those who will embrace humility and see themselves as servants.

{ *Prayer: Lord, make my heart into a humble home for you. Come dwell in me, your servant. Amen.*

Family

"Blessed be the Lord God of Israel, for he has visited and redeemed his people and has raised up a horn of salvation for us in the house of his servant David, as he spoke by the mouth of his holy prophets from of old,"
(Luke 1:68-70).

There's something innate in each one of us that longs to know our family's history. We're curious about our ancestors. We attentively listen to our parents and grandparents' stories. We ponder the details that led to our arrival. This knowledge can bring us a deep sense of belonging.

Following the birth of John, the messenger sent before Christ, Zechariah recognized his family's role in history. He knew the prophecies of his people and what God foretold. Because he knew the history, he understood the present day and felt the magnitude of what God was doing with him and his wife. His family played a major role in the greatest story ever told.

We may not know the stories of our ancestors or feel close to our earthly families, but advent means all who believe in the baby born, Jesus Christ, become part of His family. In Christ, we inherit a lineage full of people who experienced the wonder and awe of God. In God, we don't only belong, but we see we're alive in a special time in history.

{ *Prayer: Lord, help me find belonging in your family and see I've been born for a reason. Amen.*

Church

"And when the time came for their purification according to the Law of Moses, they brought him up to Jerusalem to present him to the Lord," (Luke 2:22).

It's one of the toughest commitments to make and one of the easiest to break: church. When a calendar becomes full, or our hearts flood with overwhelming emotions, it's easy to isolate and skip gatherings. Yet God longs for His children to assemble, meet and worship as a community. He wants us to get involved with a church.

Mary and Joseph, two first-time parents, undoubtedly had a lot on their plates. Yet they didn't forego gathering at the temple and following the Jewish custom of dedicating their son. This honored and pleased God. Several people even testified to God's amazing plan once they walked in. Lives were changed that day because people chose to show up in God's house.

Although we no longer live under the law, Christ wants us to gather as a church family. The places we meet may not all function the same, and our styles will be different. Some of us will meet in homes, others in gyms and auditoriums. But when Christians get together to worship and pray, we become the bride of Christ. In our faithful commitments to worship together, advent shows us we can expect to meet God.

{ *Prayer: Lord, help me not give up worshipping you in a gathering of believers. Amen.*

Waiting

"Now there was a man in Jerusalem, whose name was Simeon, and this man was righteous and devout, waiting for the consolation of Israel, and the Holy Spirit was upon him," (Luke 2:25).

Wait. It's a hard word to hear regardless of our age. Whether we're two, 22, or 82 years old, waiting is rarely easy and fun. We hate the lines. We struggle when our family is slow getting out the door. We long for a special someone at Christmas. We want to open our Christmas presents now! Not only is waiting difficult, but the familiarity of the mundane invites discontentment the longer our waiting goes on. Especially when we don't see an end in sight.

After Jesus was born, His parents took Him to the temple to dedicate and bless Him. At the temple, they met Simeon, an old man who was waiting to see the Christ before he died. In his waiting, he hadn't grown weary. He stayed alert and ready because the Holy Spirit was in Him. God helped Him wait. Once Mary and Joseph carried Jesus inside, He saw God's son. The promises were true. His wait was over.

We can easily fall into temptation during seasons of waiting. We will feel like giving up and lose hope the longer our waiting goes on. But advent reminds us of the character of God - the one who ended 40 years of wilderness and 400 years of silence preceding the birth of Christ. God helps us persevere; He promises to appear.

{ *Prayer: Lord, help me embrace my waiting and put my hope in your promise to appear. Amen.*

The Unexpected Blessing of Interruptions

Interruptions and irritations—we typically don't like them. We grumble at detours, we grit our teeth at hang-ups, we complain about snags—especially when we've carefully made plans. Yet advent shows us a different way. It guides us into embracing the annoyances, and pressing into our frustrating circumstances. It teaches us to welcome the unexpected and believe in blessings in disguise.

Communications Breakdown

"And behold, you will be silent and unable to speak until the day that these things take place, because you did not believe my words, which will be fulfilled in their time," (Luke 1:20).

We miss the memo: it was an ugly sweater party but we wore a black cocktail dress. Our kids texted, but they didn't call, and it hurts more than they know. Everyone showed up two hours late because they didn't realize the meal was at noon, and now the ham is cold. During Christmas, there's immense opportunity for communication breakdowns.

Even in the advent story, we see a breakdown in communication. When Zechariah didn't believe the angel who appeared to say his infertile wife, Elizabeth, would become pregnant, he became mute. Let's imagine being unable to speak to our spouse about seeing an angel *and* experiencing a miracle. It was likely challenging and frustrating for both of them. But this was Elizabeth's response: *"Thus the Lord has done for me in the days when he looked on me, to take away my reproach among people," (Luke 1:25).* While she could have grumbled (and may have certainly had frustrating days), she set an example of how to respond when communication breaks down— she looked to the Lord.

When we face similar breakdowns, we must look for God and find grace and patience. He will help us communicate and see beyond the circumstances and into the bigger purpose of what He's doing.

{ *Prayer: Lord, help me offer patience in communication breakdowns and show me your plans. Amen.*

Physical Struggles

"And while they were there, the time came for her to give birth," (Luke 2:6).

When our bodies are hurting, tired or weak, we can easily fall apart. Sometimes, we can control our physical struggles. We can eat healthier foods (despite the treats sitting around), exercise, prioritize sleep and drink water. Other times, we have no control. The flu virus and stomach bug show no mercy, chronic disease and recurring pain won't go away. When we don't feel well or we're uncomfortable, it's tempting to shut down, hole up and disengage.

It's a wonder how Mary felt when she traveled across the country on the back of a small donkey shortly before giving birth. A full-term, pregnant woman could likely think of many other places she'd rather be, yet Mary persisted. She pushed through physical discomfort and didn't let that stop her from the most important things. She fulfilled a critical detail of Old Testament prophecy—her baby, Christ Jesus, was born in Bethlehem.

Although it's important to rest our bodies, especially when we're sick, we must also find the strength to push through and stay alert to how God's calling us. We must take care of our bodies so we have the health to go. And we must strengthen our minds to remember we can serve Christ even when we feel weak or uncomfortable. God is healer, provider and sustainer of all things.

{ *Prayer: Lord, help me take care of my body and experience you even when I feel weak. Give me strength and stamina to obey your calling. Amen.*

Bad Timing

"Now the birth of Jesus Christ took place in this way. When his mother Mary had been betrothed to Joseph, before they came together, she was found to be with child from the Holy Spirit," (Matthew 1:18).

A loved one calls in the middle of an important meeting. A perfect job offer involves moving away from a beloved community. A prior commitment on the calendar is why the free tickets must go to someone else. It can be gut-wrenching when something good comes along at an inopportune time. The emotional middle ground of wanting good things that oppose one another is incredibly bittersweet.

Joseph and Mary likely knew this feeling immediately after they received the news a baby was on the way. Prior to the angelic encounters, they were a young, engaged couple planning their wedding and dreaming of starting a family later down the line. But their timeline got rearranged and they found themselves preparing to be parents in the midst of getting married. It may have been horrible timing for them, but it was the most perfectly-timed event in all of human history to God.

While our situations may not appear to carry the same gravity as Mary and Joseph's, we also go through times when good things seem to oppose one another. Yet advent teaches us to look for God when we face them. He has a plan and a perfect way.

{ *Prayer: Lord, give me a heavenly perspective when it feels like good things come at bad times. Amen.*

Substitutes

"And she gave birth to her firstborn son and wrapped him in swaddling cloths and laid him in a manger, because there was no place for them in the inn," (Luke 2:7).

"It's not the same." Sometimes our hearts utter this nonchalantly; we try a new recipe but learn we prefer the old. Christmas Eve service uses plastic candles instead of wax. Other times, our groans come from deeper places of loss. A loved one passes away; their presence leaves a noticeable hole. A divorce breaks traditions; a blended family tries to start anew. In loss, it can be difficult to stay open to new things and not reject what feels like a substitute.

I doubt a dirty barn full of straw is what Mary and Joseph envisioned for a birthing center, especially for the son of God. Instead of a clean cradle tucked away in their home, the couple laid their baby inside a feeding trough. Although not ideal at the time, the baby in the manger eventually showed the power of His substitute bed. He said, *"whoever drinks of the water that I will give him will never be thirsty again," (John 4:14),* and *"I am the bread of life; whoever comes to me shall not hunger, and whoever believes in me shall never thirst," (John 6:35).* In the end, the manger-turned-crib seemed fitting after all.

Grief from loss is never easy, especially during the holidays. We easily can reject suggestions or ideas of substitutes, or compare the old with the new. But advent teaches us to not give up. Sometimes the substitute is exactly what we need.

{ *Prayer: Lord, help me see that you provide what I need through any pain or loss. Amen.*

Unexpected Guests

"When the angels went away from them into heaven, the shepherds said to one another, 'Let us go over to Bethlehem and see this thing that has happened, which the Lord has made known to us,'" (Luke 2:15).

It's the person who knocks on the door because they need to decompress, pushing back bedtime. It's the last-minute request if a guest can join Christmas dinner but the package contained 12 rolls, and the new person makes 13. It's easy to view our unexpected guests and requests as stresses and burdens. But advent teaches us how to make room for people whom we weren't expecting.

The shepherds were surprised by their visitors when a group of angels showed up in the field one night. They hadn't planned on leaving their sheep to make a newborn visit, but that's what became of their evening. I doubt Mary and Joseph were expecting company as they holed up in a dirty barn and cuddled their new baby. Yet unexpected guests and unplanned encounters are weaved all throughout the Christmas story.

When we walk with Jesus, we can expect to continually face unexpected visitors and unplanned guests. The example of Christ shows us to stay open and welcome them in.

{ *Prayer: Lord, help me welcome people into my life, even if I'm not expecting them. Amen.*

Detours

*"And being warned in a dream not to return to Herod, they [the wise men]
departed to their own country by another way," (Matthew 2:12).*

Snow drifts pile high, road work reroutes traffic, unfortunate
wrecks put a halt to everyone's travel plans. We burn the dinner,
the package doesn't show up on time. Although we're familiar with
detours and "plan B's," few of us like them. Especially when we're
running late, or we get very busy.

Three wise men traveled from the far east to visit Jesus once He was
born. They followed a star as their compass, God supernaturally
provided them with a map. Yet once the visit was over, they couldn't
return home the way they came. The dangerous King Herod was
plotting to kill the newborn king; God told them in a dream to take a
detour home. God used the rerouting to protect His son and the men.

The advent story's detour reminds us to embrace the times we're led
into an unexpected direction and encounter a change of plans. God
is in the detours, oftentimes working things out for our protection.

{ *Prayer: Lord, help me embrace the plans I cannot see and view
detours as a way you protect me. Amen.*

Imperfections

"So all the generations from Abraham to David were fourteen generations, and from David to the deportation to Babylon fourteen generations, and from the deportation to Babylon to the Christ fourteen generations,"
(Matthew 1:17).

I descend from imperfect ancestors, I bet you do too. Our family trees are full of people who've made bad choices and said hurtful words. The people we eat with around our tables during Christmas dinner have all made terrible mistakes. There's nothing like a holiday to trigger hard feelings and old memories of pain. It's hard to descend from imperfect people.

Our family trees are not unlike the family tree of Jesus. His lineage shows his earthly ancestors were a lot like ours. From Abraham to Jacob, Rahab to David, there's a line of people with good, bad and ugly stories. Yet these people were not beyond the grace of God, and He used them to bring His perfect son into the world and demonstrate that anyone can receive total forgiveness, redemption and freedom. Anyone can be used by God.

As we get together with our loved ones for Christmas, may we ask God for a heart that sees our imperfect relatives like He does—people worthy of love, forgiveness and kindness. We're not perfect, nor are they. The advent story is for all of us, nobody is exempt from the invitation to dine at God's table and adore His son.

{ *Prayer: Lord, help me love my family members despite their imperfections and shortcomings. Help me forgive them for my pain. Amen.*

The Unexpected Power of Adoration

As the twinkling lights and soft notes from familiar carols float through the winter air, the atmosphere changes. While all year long, we offer prayers, do our studies, and sing out praises, advent invites us to experience more. It's an invitation into something deeper we didn't know was there. As we gaze upon a miracle baby in a story only God could write, we step into the transforming power of adoration. As we kneel at the side of the manger, we're changed.

Perfect Gift

"The Spirit of the Lord God is upon me, because the Lord has anointed me to bring good news to the poor; he has sent me to bind up the brokenhearted, to proclaim liberty to the captives, and the opening of the prison to those who are bound," (Isaiah 61:1).

Leading up to Christmas, many children suddenly drop poor behavior and become wonderfully-behaved little kids all because of a simple threat: coal. Fighting and bickering slows, bad attitudes turn around. Nobody wants to experience Christmas morning without gorgeous presents under their tree. The powerful thing is that loving parents don't actually give their children handfuls of soot (even if their behavior warrants it).

The Israelites weren't too unlike kids who act out in ways that technically warrant receiving coal for Christmas. They fought, disagreed, turned to false idols and disobeyed. As God's children today, we still act out in these ways. When sin gets the best of us, we ignore God and hurt others. Our actions don't line up with how He's called us to live. Yet during advent, we celebrate the birth of Christ—a gift always ready for us to unwrap. Jesus means we'll never get "coal."

As the children of God, we don't get what we deserve, but we receive Jesus Christ. He is a gift that will never end, no matter how many times we mess up and regardless of our bad behavior. He is a gift that sets us free.

{ *Prayer: Lord, thank you that I don't get what I deserve, but for sending the perfect gift, Jesus. Amen.*

Answers

"But the angel said to him, 'Do not be afraid, Zechariah, for your prayer has been heard, and your wife Elizabeth will bear you a son, and you shall call his name John,'" (Luke 1:13).

It can be painful to say the prayers we said yesterday. And the day before. Fewer things challenge our faith than, what appears to be, unanswered prayers. When our relationships don't change, our jobs fall through, we don't conceive or get our way, we struggle. Our flesh grows disappointed and our minds tell us to stop praying.

For years, Zechariah and Elizabeth longed for a child, yet they couldn't conceive. But one day, God opened Elizabeth's womb and they became pregnant with John. God answered the longing of their hearts, although it took many years. Through days and nights of unanswered prayers, they stayed faithful to ask, worship and serve the Lord.

Our answers to prayer will not always come as literally as Elizabeth's, although they may. The advent story shows us to never stop asking God for our heart's desires. God cares about our hopes and dreams. He is listening. In His perfect timing, and His perfect way, He will answer us.

{ *Prayer: Lord, help me not give up praying for what seems to be impossible. Amen.*

A Quiet Heart

"My soul magnifies the Lord, and my spirit rejoices in God my Savior, for he has looked on the humble estate of his servant. For behold, from now on all generations will call me blessed," (Luke 1:46-48).

Some of the most popular Christmas songs hit on it: it's not the big, flashy gifts but the quiet displays of genuine love that we long for the most. It's the Christmas shoes bought with a little wad of cash or the doorbell ringing because a loved one is surprising us. While big, red bows and shiny new toys are fun, our hearts fill up the most when we experience the simplicity of love.

Upon realizing that out of all of the females God could have chosen to carry His son, Mary didn't puff up and tout the news around town. She didn't alert the media nor did she wave her chosen position in front of all to see. Mary's quiet and humble heart responded in line with her character. She worshipped God and adored Him for such a holy calling. Her worship led her into a relationship with Him like none other.

In a culture that celebrates "go big or go home," we will find our hearts most at home when we imitate Mary's response. May we identify ourselves as humble servants and in the quiet spaces, experience the true reason for the holidays.

{ *Prayer: Lord, help me look past the hype of the holiday and enter the secret place with you. Amen.*

Mindfulness

"And her husband Joseph, being a just man and unwilling to put her to shame, resolved to divorce her quietly. But as he considered these things, behold, an angel of the Lord appeared to him in a dream, saying, 'Joseph, son of David, do not fear to take Mary as your wife, for that which is conceived in her is from the Holy Spirit,'" (Matthew 1:19-20).

We've all done it. We sit on the couch and stew over yet another family obligation. We judge our co-workers for eating too many crackers and sausages, or for having one too many drinks. We check our watches at church and daydream about lunch. We're oblivious to our thoughts, and that God knows them.

One night after the angel visited Joseph and told him his fiancée Mary was pregnant, yet not with his child but God's child, he couldn't make sense of it. Who could? We can read between the lines of the story and gather that his thoughts took off in a million directions. Yet we also see that God knew his thoughts, intervened to help him process them through a dream, and revealed his next step and calling.

As human beings, we all have thoughts that cross our minds every second of the day. Our minds are built to mull over our experiences— the good and the bad—when we're both awake and sleeping. Advent reminds us that God cares and knows about our thoughts; He can help us capture and surrender them all to Him. Mindfulness can align us with God's plans.

{ *Prayer: Lord, help me become aware of the secret thoughts of my mind and lead me to my next step. Amen.*

Giftedness

*"She did not depart from the temple, worshiping with fasting and prayer
night and day. And coming up at that very hour, she began to give
thanks to God and to speak of him to all who were waiting
for the redemption of Jerusalem," (Luke 2:37-38).*

Do you have someone in your family who makes a favorite recipe
each year? One of my aunts is gifted at baking homemade rolls
and sugar cookies. While technically she could make these recipes
any time of the year, she usually waits for the holidays to bake them.
We think everything tastes better at Christmas.

On the tail end of the story about Jesus' birth, we meet Anna. An
84-year-old widow, she was known to be at the temple praying and
worshipping each day and night. When Mary and Joseph walked in to
dedicate Jesus, her heart became so full, she began to explain who the
child was, and his God-given purpose. Her gifts shined through.

Because of her prepared heart and nearness to the Lord, Anna's
gifting came out. She encouraged, taught and affirmed the people
around her. As we draw close to the baby in the manger during
advent, we can expect and hope for God's gifts to also arise in us,
allowing us to love and bless others.

{ *Prayer: Lord, fill me with your Spirit and let the gifts you've put
in me be used to share about you. Amen.*

Honor

"And going into the house, they saw the child with Mary his mother, and they fell down and worshiped him. Then, opening their treasures, they offered him gifts, gold and frankincense and myrrh," (Matthew 2:11).

Why exchange gifts? What's the point of presents? It's usually only a few days before Christmas when the stress of wrapping every package and purchasing last-minute gifts becomes overwhelming. I question the tradition of gift giving. In a world that survives off of unhealthy consumerism, I grow disappointed and fearful I'm part of the problem until I remember the power of a gift.

In most nativity sets around the world, three ornately-dressed men holding presents surround baby Jesus. The gifts aren't toys or diapers, but spices and perfumes—odd offerings for a newborn, yet significant displays of honor. The wise men followed a star in the sky, and by the same guiding light, they knew just what to bring. The gifts honored the baby, his family, and the special role God planned for Him.

The wise men remind us that gifts bring honor. Gifts show others they're valuable to us. They send a message that someone is worthy of love. They don't need to be big or expensive, or even tangible at times. Gifts allow us to love and honor one another.

{ *Prayer: Lord, help me honor others with my gifts, and receive honor when others give gifts to me. Amen.*

- Day 21 -

Wonder

"And suddenly there was with the angel a multitude of the heavenly host praising God and saying, 'Glory to God in the highest, and on earth peace among those with whom he is pleased!'" (Luke 2:13-14).

I love it when neighbors get together and put up grandiose Christmas light displays. When not one, but multiple houses, along a street string up colorful lights and blow up inflatable outdoor displays, it's beautiful. A magical sense of wonder takes over.

This must be a tiny picture of what it was like for the shepherds when a heavenly host appeared and declared "glory to God" in unison. A choir of angels all speaking and singing one message would have certainly put goosebumps on their arms and widened their eyes. No wonder they left their sheep and took off to find the baby immediately. What a magical, fun experience it must have been in the fields that night.

The invitation to join the heavenly host and worship our Lord together still exists. We may not see the angel choirs with our eyes until we get to Heaven, but advent reminds us that our voices are part of a large, beautiful chorus full of all of God's creation worshiping the newborn king.

{ *Prayer: Lord, help me join my voice with others on earth and in heaven worshiping Jesus today. Amen.*

The Unexpected Promises of God

The promise of God is love. It's unending grace and forgiveness. It's the total elimination of death and darkness. It's the promise of light. Each year we celebrate advent because God keeps his promises—no matter how dark things may seem. Just as faithful as the trees that dropped fall leaves plan to regrow them in spring, God will come through for us. Even if we don't expect it.

Impossible Becomes Possible

"For nothing will be impossible with God," (Luke 1:37).

Google it. We live in a world where the answer to most of life's complex questions is just a few taps away. We're stuck on reasoning and explaining all of life's mysteries. How did the magician do the trick? How did the butterfly transform? How did the underdog army defeat the all-powerful enemy? Just search for the answer, it's seconds away and most likely a YouTube video as well.

Yet when we pause to honor advent, we're reminded of two things. One, there are still situations that render impossible on earth. While reason and information makes us feel like we can do and know everything, life still has limits and limitations. Some things simply cannot be, and simply cannot be known.

Two, God takes our limits and breaks them. From a virgin woman becoming a mom to stars appearing in the sky and serving as a holy compass, advent reminds us that what man cannot do, God can. He is a God of miracles, and He promises that what is impossible for us is possible with Him.

{ *Prayer: Lord, help me believe that all things are possible with you. Amen.*

God With Us

"Behold, the virgin shall conceive and bear a son, and they shall call his name Immanuel," (Matthew 1:23).

4oo years - can you imagine it? To put it in perspective, around 400 years ago, the United States was colonized. Pocahontas was alive, the first slaves were brought into North America, and the pilgrims wrote the Mayflower Compact. That's a long time! Yet 400 years is how long the Jewish people looked for a savior God promised through the prophets, yet heard nothing.

The birth of Jesus broke the 400 "silent years" with an announcement of "Immanuel," God with us. The baby in the manger was the savior they'd waited for—God in the flesh dwelling amongst them. The baby grew up into a man who lived, ate and walked amongst the people. His message was one of love and grace; He was the light of the world.

Today, thousands of years have passed since Jesus was born. Yet never again has God gone silent. After He left earth, Jesus sent the Holy Spirit to dwell amongst us. Now, He lives in our hearts. Advent reminds us that forever God is with us—Immanuel.

{ *Prayer: Lord, help me see and feel that you are with me today. Amen.*

Love

"In this the love of God was made manifest among us, that God sent his only Son into the world, so that we might live through him," (1 John 4:9).

Why do we host the holidays? Why do we attend parties and close the office? Why do we purchase gifts and cook yummy dinners? Why go to all of this work and expense? We do it because of **love.**

Advent is the celebration of love. The baby in the manger was a gift from heaven so all people could know and experience this phenomenon—God loves us. It's something so big and so majestic— to be loved so personally and deeply despite our flaws. It's nearly unfathomable. But God tucked this love inside of a baby. And because He did, most of us can start to wrap our brains around this miracle. The creator of the world loves us.

To know God is to know love. To experience God is to experience love. God is the biggest sensation, the most true version of total love, we will find here on earth. This love is why we endure the stress and pain of the holidays. It's why we fight through depression and disappointments. It's why we open our homes and our hearts. It's why we give and receive. Love is God's great promise to us.

{ *Prayer: Lord, help me experience and know you are love. Amen.*

Light of Life

*"Again Jesus spoke to them, saying, 'I am the light of the world.
Whoever follows me will not walk in darkness, but will have
the light of life,'" (John 8:12).*

The glow of white lights piercing a midnight sky takes my breath away. I admire them even more when I know that against chilly winds and shaky ladders, people climbed high to staple strings against houses and buildings. Bulb after bulb full of brightness and color, the lights are carefully placed for such a time as this. With each twinkle, I feel happy. I feel safe. The dark night isn't so dark anymore.

Advent is the story of Jesus leaving heaven for earth. He faced danger, abuse, struggle and suffering so God's light would shine into our hearts and remove our darkness. Full of love and hope, He knew we needed Him. He is the light of life.

Jesus enters our mundane so we notice the gravity of His arrival. He interrupts our plans so we don't miss it when He arrives. He transforms our ongoing rhythms of life into deeper understandings of adoration. He sends sweet reminders of His promises. When and where we encounter Him, we won't always know. But we can be sure that the light of advent will always be shining, even when we least expect it.

{ *Prayer: Lord, thank you that the light of life never goes out. Amen.*

-

 Danielle Ripley-Burgess is a two-time colon cancer survivor first diagnosed at age 17. She lives in the Kansas City area and blogs about cancer survivorship, faith and family. She writes and speaks to encourage those facing trials and suffering under a motto of "faith that survives." She married her high school sweetheart, Mike, and adopted her beautiful daughter, Mae. Her personal story has been told around the world through newspaper articles, blogs, TV and radio shows including The Today Show, BBC's World Have Your Say, Sirius Radio's Doctor Radio, The Chicago Tribune, among others. She's published several devotionals and articles, and she guest blogs on many websites. When she's not writing, she can be found baking her favorite chocolate chip cookie recipe. It's a good one.

Read more at *DanielleRipleyBurgess.com*
Follow along on Twitter at *@DanielleisB*

Made in the USA
Monee, IL
28 November 2019